·TELL ME ABOUT·

FLOWERS TREES & OTHER PLANTS

SERIES EDITOR: JACKIE GAFF

Warwick Press

Published in 1991 by Warwick Press,
387 Park Avenue South, New York, N.Y. 10016.
First published in 1991 by Kingfisher Books.
Copyright © Grisewood & Dempsey Ltd. 1991.

Printed in Spain

Library of Congress Cataloging-in-Publication Data
Royston, Angela.
    Flowers, trees, and other plants / Angela
Royston.
       p.   cm.—(Tell me about)
    Includes index.
    Summary: Studies the highly visible and
diverse world of trees, flowers, and other green-
and-growing things, with their distinct ways of
reproduction, respiration, photosynthesis, and
nourishment. Includes suggestions for projects
and activities.
    ISBN 0-531-19110-9
    1. Plants—Miscellanea—Juvenile literature.
[1. Plants—Miscellanea. 2. Questions and
answers.] I. Title. II. Series: Tell me about
(Warwick Press)
QK49.R69 1991
581—dc20   90-12994
                                    CIP
                                     AC

Contents

What are plants like?   4

Which plant has the biggest
    flowers?   6

Which plant has the largest
    leaves?   6

Which are the biggest plants?   7

How do plants use sunlight?   8

Which plants grow in the air?   9

Why do plants have flowers?   10

Why are flowers brightly
    colored?   11

What is a fruit?   12

How do animals help plants?   13

Why do some fruits have wings? 13

How do seeds grow? 14

Can new plants grow without seeds? 15

Can plants eat animals? 16

Why do some plants scratch and sting? 17

Why do trees shed their leaves? 18

How do trees grow? 20

What lives in an oak tree? 21

Which tree can make a forest? 22

Which tree swells? 22

Which trees grow on stilts? 23

Which trees travel the oceans? 23

How do we use trees? 24

Which plants don't have flowers? 26

Are fungi plants? 27

Can plants grow in water? 28

Which plants grow in the sea? 28

Can plants grow without water? 29

What plant grows in rainforests? 30

Can plants grow in the snow? 31

Which plants do we eat? 32

Which plants do we drink? 34

How is cotton made? 35

Which were the first plants? 36

Why do some plants die out? 38

Useful words 39

Index 40

What are plants like?

There are thousands of different plants in the world, and they come in an amazing variety of shapes, colors, and sizes—from tiny algae which can only be seen under a microscope to huge trees more than 300 feet tall.

All these different sorts of plants have one thing in common—they make their own food using the energy in sunlight. Animals cannot do this, so they have to hunt around for food to eat instead.

Scientists have named more than 350,000 species, or types, of plants, dividing them into two main groups—those that produce flowers and those that don't. More than two-thirds of all plants belong to the flowering group.

 DO YOU KNOW

Plants grow in almost every part of the world, and different species are able to survive the harshest climates. Some plants manage to grow on the cold snowy slopes of the highest mountains. Others can survive and even flower in hot dry deserts where it hardly ever rains.

Grass species include wheat, corn, and rice, which provide most of the world's food. Grasses are flowering plants.

Mosses are non-flowering plants. Most species grow in damp shady places—near streams, for example, or in woods.

Trees belong to the flowering plant group. Scientists have named around 20,000 different tree species.

PLANT FACTS

● All flowering plants have the same four main parts: roots, stems, leaves, and flowers. They reproduce, or make new plants, by growing seeds. A seed is a tiny capsule with a baby plant inside it.

Flower

Stem

Leaf

Root

Bracken is a type of fern which grows in woodland and on hill-sides. Ferns are non-flowering plants.

Different flowering plants bloom throughout the year. Some produce a single flower. Others have many tiny blossoms.

● Non-flowering plants don't have flowers and can't make seeds. Instead, they reproduce by making spores. A spore is a tiny cell, and a cell is the smallest living part of a plant or an animal.

Seaweeds are non-flowering plants which grow in water or in damp shady places.

Which plant has the biggest flowers?

The biggest flower in the world belongs to a strange plant called Rafflesia, which grows in Southeast Asia. The Rafflesia's gigantic flower can measure up to 3 feet across, and weigh as much as 15 pounds—about the same as a 6-month-old baby!

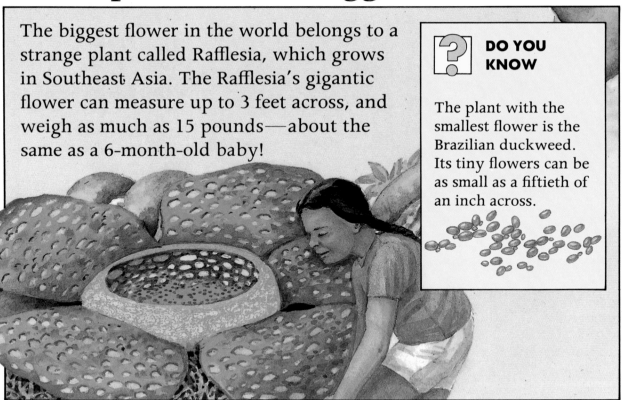

Which plant has the largest leaves?

The leaves of South America's giant Victoria water lily are among the world's largest—they can measure more than 6 feet across. Some are strong enough to remain floating even when supporting the weight of a small child!

Raffia palms grow in Madagascar

Which are the biggest plants?

The world's biggest plants are trees, and the tree height record is held by a species of Australian eucalyptus which can grow to be more than 370 feet high.

The biggest and heaviest trees in the world are the giant sequoias. The largest contains around 6,100 tons of wood—enough to make more than 5 billion matches! It's called General Sherman, after a famous U.S. army officer.

? DO YOU KNOW

The world's fattest tree is a species of cypress which measures 36 feet across the base of its trunk. It's called a Montezuma cypress and it grows in Mexico. It would take 20 people holding hands to encircle it!

Forests of giant sequoias once grew all over the northern half of the world. Today, they are only found in the Sierra Nevada mountains of California.

The giant sequoia General Sherman is nearly 275 feet high. It is thought to be between 2,200 and 2,500 years old.

Giant trees need massive trunks to support them. General Sherman's measures over 30 feet across.

How do plants use sunlight?

Plants use sunlight to make food in their leaves, through a process called photosynthesis. Their leaves contain a special green substance called chlorophyll which can capture the energy in sunlight. This energy is then used to turn water from the soil and carbon dioxide gas from the air into a sugary food.

? DO YOU KNOW

Plants are essential to life on Earth because they give out the oxygen gas that we and other animals breathe to stay alive. Oxygen is the waste product given off by plants after they've made their food using sunlight.

3 Plants take in the carbon dioxide gas they use in photosynthesis through their stomata. These are tiny holes on the underside of the leaves. The plants give out oxygen gas.

4 The food that is made in the leaves is carried in a watery sap to all parts of the plant.

Oxygen is given out

Sunlight enters

Carbon dioxide enters

2 The water flows up the stem to the leaves through narrow tubes called xylem.

1 A network of fine roots spreads through the soil to find and take in water.

Which plants grow in the air?

In the hot, damp tropical forests of South America, plants such as orchids and bromeliads grow high up in the branches of trees. They grow in tiny pockets of soil that form in bark. Their roots dangle freely and they take in most of the moisture they need from the air. These air plants are known as epiphytes.

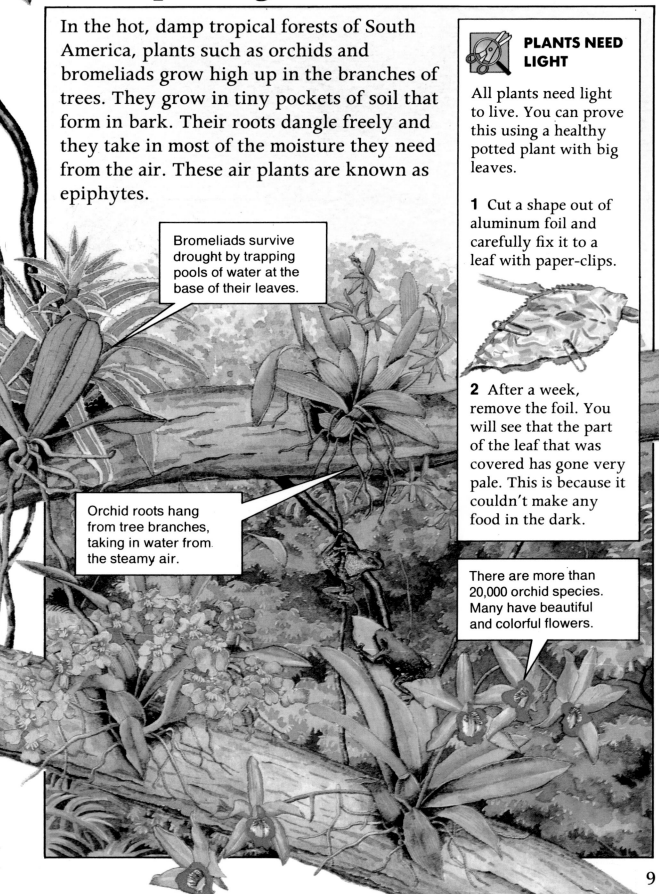

Bromeliads survive drought by trapping pools of water at the base of their leaves.

Orchid roots hang from tree branches, taking in water from the steamy air.

PLANTS NEED LIGHT

All plants need light to live. You can prove this using a healthy potted plant with big leaves.

1 Cut a shape out of aluminum foil and carefully fix it to a leaf with paper-clips.

2 After a week, remove the foil. You will see that the part of the leaf that was covered has gone very pale. This is because it couldn't make any food in the dark.

There are more than 20,000 orchid species. Many have beautiful and colorful flowers.

Why do plants have flowers?

As well as looking pretty and smelling good, flowers have a very imporant job to do. They make the seeds that grow into new plants. Most flowers have the same main male and female parts. The male parts are called stamens and they produce pollen grains. The femals parts are called carpels, and they are made up of a stigma, a style, and an ovary. Ovaries are where eggs are made. A new seed is formed when a pollen grain joins with an egg, in a process called fertilization.

POLLEN FACTS

● The largest pollen grains are only a hundreth of an inch across—smaller than a period in this book.

● One catkin, or flower, of the birch tree can make up to 5.5 million pollen grains.

Birch catkin

1 The stigma is at the top of the carpel. It's sticky, which helps it to catch pollen grains.

2 This part of the carpel is called the style. The pollen grains travel down it.

3 Each ovary contains an egg. A new seed grows after the egg joins with a pollen grain.

Stamens are the male parts of a flower and they produce pollen grains. Most plants have a number of stamens.

Why are flowers brightly colored?

Flowers are brightly colored to attract insects and other animals to them. These animal visitors are important because they help with fertilization by carrying pollen from one plant to another. Plants produce pollen in their own stamens, of course. However, their eggs are usually fertilized by pollen from another plant.

DO YOU KNOW

Not all flowers smell good. The stapelia flower (above) reeks of rotting meat! Although horrible to us, it smells like a delicious meal to flies that eat rotting meat. They are tricked into visiting the flower, and collect pollen at the same time.

1 Many birds and insects visit flowers to feed on nectar, a sweet liquid made at the base of the petals.

3 When it visits another flower, some of the pollen may rub off onto the stigma at the top of the carpel.

2 As the animal feeds, it rubs against the stamens and pollen grains stick to its body.

The tiny Australian honey possum is an unusual flower visitor. Most of the animals that carry pollen have wings and can fly!

What is a fruit?

A fruit is the part of a plant that protects new seeds as they grow. The plant's ovaries develop into fruit once the eggs inside them have been fertilized by pollen grains.

Seed

Seed

Some plants produce fleshy fruits which are juicy and good to eat—apples, pears, and oranges, for example. Others produce dry fruits such as nuts or pea pods.

 FRUIT AND NUT FACTS

• The jackfruit grows in southern Asia and produces the largest fruit in the world. One fruit can weigh up to 65 pounds—heavier than a 7-year-old child!

Jackfruit trees have the heaviest fruit

• The world's largest nut is produced by the coco-de-mer tree, which grows only in the Seychelles. These are a group of islands in the Indian Ocean. Each of the huge nuts can weigh as much as 40 pounds and take six years to ripen.

How do animals help plants?

Animals help plants by spreading seeds to places where growing conditions are good. Some seeds are carried on animals' coats. Others are swallowed when animals eat the fleshy fruits that protect them. The hard seeds travel through the animals' bodies unharmed.

SEEDS ON YOUR FEET

Did you know that you sometimes help plants by spreading seeds? After a country walk, try scraping the mud from your shoes on to some soil in a seed tray. Keep the soil warm and damp. Watch to see what grows.

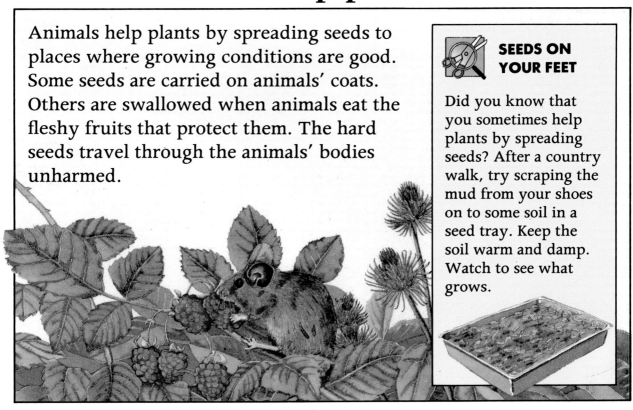

Why do some fruits have wings?

Some fruits are specially designed to be spread by the wind, and have wings or feathery parachutes to help them fly. Heavier seeds float gently to the ground, but lighter ones can be carried huge distances.

Sycamore trees produce winged fruits which spin through the air like helicopters.

Dandelion seeds can float through the air for long distances on their hairy parachutes.

How do seeds grow?

Every seed has the tiny beginnings of a new plant inside it. This germinates, or starts to grow, when the ground is warm enough and the seed has enough water. There is a store of food inside the seed to keep the young plant growing until it can open its leaves and make its own food.

1 The seed takes in water and swells. The first root grows out.

2 Tiny hairs grow from the root and take in water.

3 The first shoot appears and grows leaves. The plant can now make its own food.

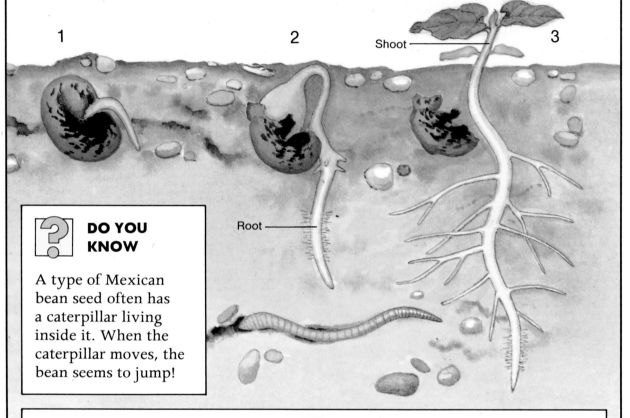

1   2   Shoot   3

Root

DO YOU KNOW

A type of Mexican bean seed often has a caterpillar living inside it. When the caterpillar moves, the bean seems to jump!

WHICH WAY IS UP?

In most flowering plants, roots always grow down and shoots always grow up.

1 Line a glass jar with blotting paper. Put bean seeds between the paper and the glass.

2 Put the jar in a warm place and keep the blotting paper damp. See how long it takes for the first root and shoot to appear.

3 Turn the jar on its side and leave it. Which way do the roots and shoots grow now?

Can new plants grow without seeds?

Many plants can reproduce without using seeds. Some have special parts which are used as food stores in the winter and grow into new plants the next year. The daffodil does this, and so does the potato. Other plants send out shoots, called runners, which become separate plants.

 DO YOU KNOW

Banana plants don't have seeds. Farmers cut off a part of the underground stem and use it to grow a new plant.

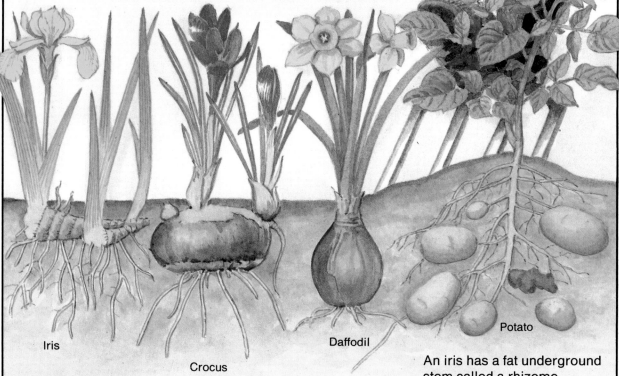

Iris

Crocus

Daffodil

Potato

An iris has a fat underground stem called a rhizome. Leaves and flowers grow from it.

A crocus flower and leaves grow from a corm, a round stem full of stored food.

A daffodil bulb is made of fleshy leaves full of food which is used by the growing shoot.

The potato we eat is a swollen part of the underground stem, which grows into a new plant.

Strawberries send out side shoots called runners. Where they touch the ground, roots form. New leaves then grow and the runner dies away.

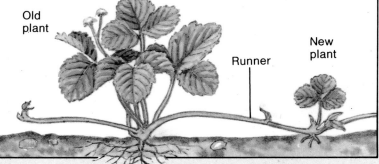

Old plant

Runner

New plant

Can plants eat animals?

Quite a few plants have special ways of trapping and eating insects and other small animals. Most of these meat-eating plants grow in places with poor soils, and they catch and eat animals to get extra food. The animals are tricked into deadly traps, where their bodies are turned into a liquid which the plant soaks up.

The pitcher plant (below) has vase-shaped leaves which are full of liquid. Insects slide off the slippery rim and drown in the pool below.

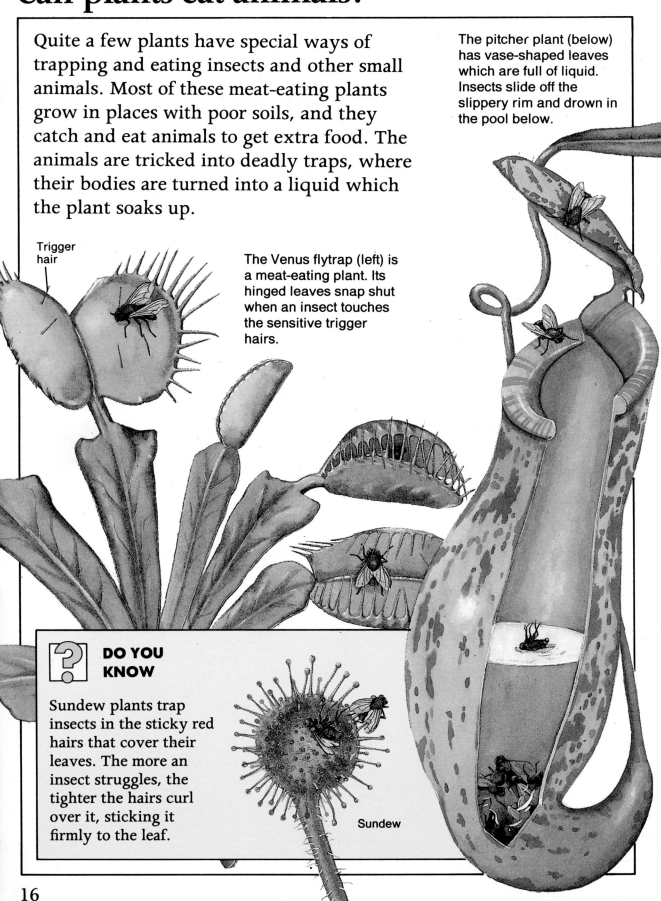

Trigger hair

The Venus flytrap (left) is a meat-eating plant. Its hinged leaves snap shut when an insect touches the sensitive trigger hairs.

? DO YOU KNOW

Sundew plants trap insects in the sticky red hairs that cover their leaves. The more an insect struggles, the tighter the hairs curl over it, sticking it firmly to the leaf.

Sundew

Why do some plants scratch and sting?

Plants scratch and sting to stop animals eating them. Unlike animals, plants don't have legs or wings to help them escape from their enemies! So they have developed special weapons to protect themselves. Plants such as cacti and thorn trees have sharp spines to keep animals away. Other plants are covered in stinging hairs.

DO YOU KNOW

The sensitive mimosa plant hates being touched. If it is stroked, its leaves fold up and the stalks droop. This may be a way of shaking off insect enemies. The mimosa also folds its leaves to protect them against the cold at night and the hot sun.

DO YOU KNOW

Each tiny hollow hair of a stinging nettle has a pool of poison at its base. When the hair's needlelike tip pierces your skin, it breaks and poison flows into the cut.

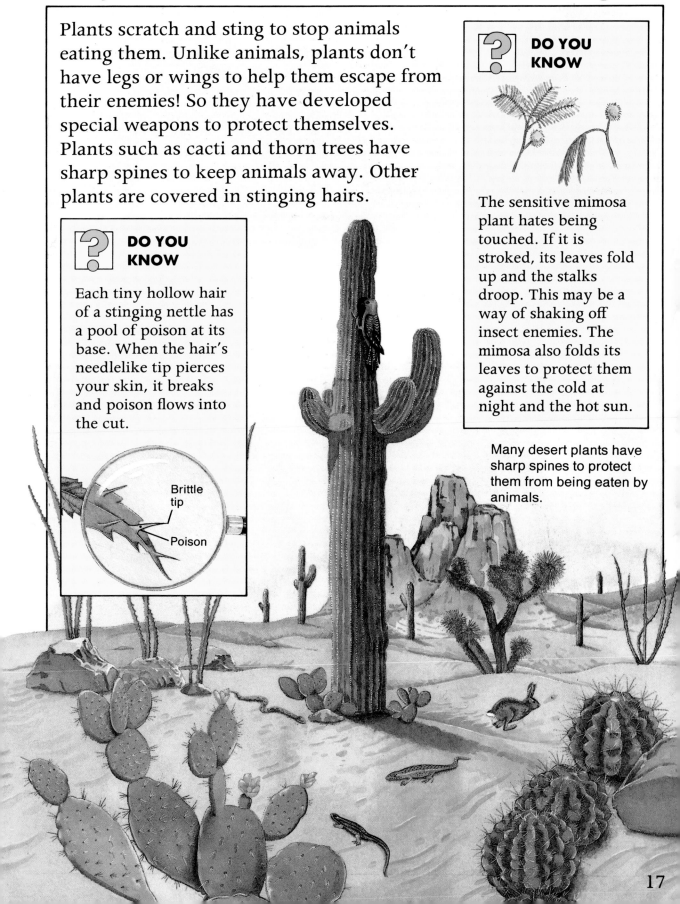

Brittle tip

Poison

Many desert plants have sharp spines to protect them from being eaten by animals.

Why do trees shed their leaves?

Trees shed their leaves each year to protect themselves against harsh winter weather. If they didn't do this, their leaves would be damaged by wind and frost. During severe frosts, trees would lose more water through their leaves than they could take up from the ground through their roots.

Not all trees shed their leaves each year, of course. The ones that do are called deciduous. Trees that don't lose their leaves are called evergreen.

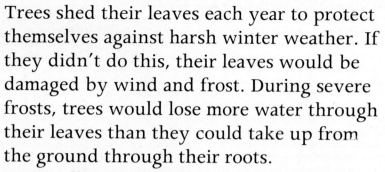

Pine

Fir

Elm

Willow

Most evergreen trees have needlelike leaves with tough waxy coats to keep water in. Each leaf lives for a few years before it's shed. Pines and firs are evergreen.

Elms, willows, and oaks are deciduous broad-leaved trees. Most broad-leaved trees grow in areas with warm summers and cool winters.

Oak

The main job of the leaves is to make food for the tree through photosynthesis. They also give off the gas oxygen and "sweat" water.

Branches spread the leaves wide to catch the sunlight needed in photosynthesis. An oak tree may have as many as a quarter of a million leaves.

WEATHER FORECAST

You can use a fir cone to tell the weather. On dry days, the cone's scales are open. In damp weather they close up tightly.

Damp weather

Dry weather

The trunk is the tree's stem. It's lined with tiny tubes which carry water from the roots to the leaves. An outer skin of bark protects the trunk.

The roots anchor the tree in the ground and take in water that the tree uses to make its food.

Palm trees form a third tree group. Most have large fan-shaped or feathery leaves but no branches. Palms grow in countries where the weather is warm all year round.

19

How do trees grow?

Trees grow and get bigger in three ways—upward, downward, and outward. They get taller as the twigs at the ends of the branches grow longer. At the same time, the roots spread deeper and wider to anchor the tree firmly in the soil. Trees get fatter each year by adding a layer of new wood just beneath the bark.

TREE FACTS

● The oldest trees in the world are the bristlecone pines (below), some of which live for more than 4,000 years. The oldest is over 4,600 years old!

● The fastest growing trees are a species of Australian eucalypt. These trees can grow more than 35 feet taller in a year!

If you look at a tree stump, you'll see rings of wood. Counting them tells you the tree's age. It grows a ring each year.

In a good year, with lots of sun and rain, the tree grows quickly and the ring is wide. A thin ring forms when the weather is bad.

What lives in an oak tree?

Trees provide food and homes for a huge number of animals. A single oak may support as many as 400 different species! Around half of these animals are insects which swarm in their thousands all over the tree, feeding on every part—leaves, bark, roots, sap, flowers, and fruits!

Insects feed on all parts of the tree. But all sorts of birds and spiders feed on the insects!

 BARK RUBBING

The pattern on the bark of a tree is like a fingerprint—each tree has its own unique pattern. Here's a way to take tree "fingerprints."

1 Hold a sheet of thick paper firmly against a tree trunk. Rub over the paper with a crayon until the bark pattern shows.

2 See how many bark patterns you can collect. You could use them to make greeting cards or as posters for your walls.

Woodpeckers live in holes which they make in the trunk. Other birds build nests high up in the branches.

Insects and worms feed among the fallen leaves and are themselves food for other small animals such as mice.

Which tree can make a forest?

The Banyan tree of India and Sri Lanka grows so many branches that it looks like a small forest. The branches have hanging supports which grow down to the ground, take root, and become new trunks. These new trunks produce new branches, and the tree gets bigger and bigger!

These trunks started off as hanging roots which grew down from the branches above.

? DO YOU KNOW

One of the largest banyan trees in the world grows in the Botanical Gardens in Calcutta, India. It has more than 1,000 trunks and covers an area of 170,000 square feet—that's far bigger than a large football field!

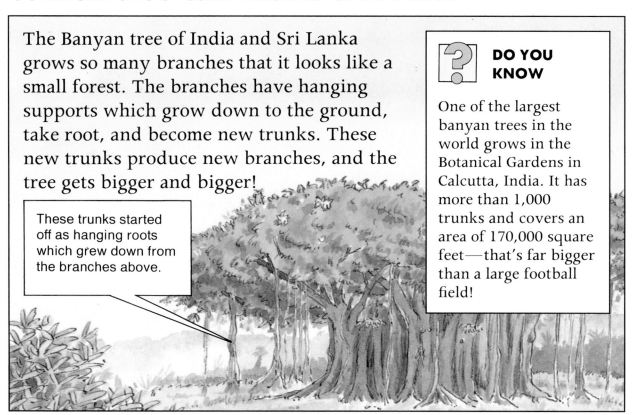

Which tree swells?

The baobab tree of Africa and Australia is unusual because its trunk shrinks and swells as the weather changes. When the rains come, it takes in water and its trunk swells and becomes huge. In times of drought, the trunk shrinks.

? DO YOU KNOW

The baobab's fruit is called monkey bread. It's about a foot long and it hangs from the tree on a long rope-like stem. Each fruit contains a number of seeds in a fleshy pulp.

Which trees grow on stilts?

Mangrove trees grow in hot tropical countries, in the salty tidal water of river mouths. Some species grow strong stiltlike roots which arch out from their branches to anchor the trees firmly in the muddy river bed.

There's hardly any oxygen in muddy water, so mangroves have special breathing roots which stick up into the air.

? **DO YOU KNOW**

Mudskippers are strange fish which can breathe in air as well as in water. They live among mangrove roots and haul themselves out of the water at low tide. They hop and wriggle up the roots using their front fins to pull themselves forward.

Which trees travel the oceans?

Coconuts float across the oceans, sometimes traveling thousands of miles. They are the fruit of a type of palm tree which often grows along the tropical island beaches. When the coconut falls from the tree, it sometimes rolls into the ocean and is carried away by the waves.

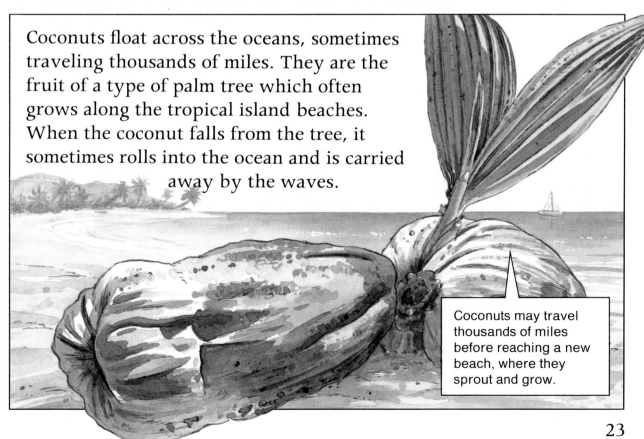

Coconuts may travel thousands of miles before reaching a new beach, where they sprout and grow.

How do we use trees?

Trees are one of the Earth's most useful natural products. Because wood is strong and lasts for a long time, we use it in building and to make a range of goods, from furniture to musical instruments.

Many of the things we eat and drink come from trees. As well as fruits and nuts, trees give us coffee and chocolate, for example.

Trees are cut down with powerful chainsaws, then taken to a sawmill. In some areas, the logs are floated down river.

At the sawmill, the logs are cut into shorter lengths. Their ends are trimmed and they are sliced up into planks.

WOOD FACTS

● Of all the trees cut down, half are burned for fuel, one third are used for sawn timber, and one sixth are used to make paper.

● We are cutting down forests seven times more quickly than we are replanting them. One way of saving trees is to reuse and recycle as much paper as possible.

Which plants don't have flowers?

Algae, mosses, and ferns are the main plant groups that don't have flowers and therefore can't make seeds. Instead they produce spores. These are single microscopic cells, with protective coats to help them survive drought and cold weather. Spores are small and light, and they can float on water or on the wind.

? **DO YOU KNOW**

Algae are the simplest form of plant life on Earth. Some are just a single cell. Others are larger—seaweeds, for example—but even large algae never have true stems, roots, or leaves. Most types of algae live in water— in rivers, ponds, and oceans. But they also grow in damp soil and on the trunks of trees.

Horsetails were among the first land plants to appear on Earth. They are distant relatives of ferns.

Underneath the fern's leaves are little brown spots. These contain the tiny spores which will grow into plants.

Mosses are found in almost all parts of the world, from the icy cold of the Poles to hot tropical forests.

Are fungi plants?

Fungi aren't really plants at all. Unlike true plants they don't have any chlorophyll and can't make their own food using sunlight. Instead, they steal their food from other plants and animals. The simplest fungi are the molds that grow on rotting food. Other kinds include the yeasts we use to bake bread, and mushrooms and toadstools.

DO YOU KNOW

Penicillin is a powerful medicine which is used to fight disease and kill germs in our bodies. It was first discovered in a small fungus called *Penicillium* (below).

Puff-balls are round. An average-sized giant puff-ball can be as big as a basketball!

The fly agaric toadstool is very poisonous. Its juice was once used to kill flies.

DEADLY POISON

Never eat or even touch any mushrooms or toadstools you find on walks. Fungi come in all shapes and sizes. Some are good to eat and have been used in recipes and medicines for hundreds of years. But many are poisonous and could even kill you.

Chanterelle mushrooms are funnel-shaped. They smell of apricots.

Bracket fungus grows out of the trunks of living and dead trees like a bracket or shelf.

Can plants grow in water?

Several kinds of plant grow in the shallow water along the edges of ponds and streams. They have strong roots to fix them firmly in the mud. There are also plants which grow partly or completely covered by water. Others float freely on the water's surface.

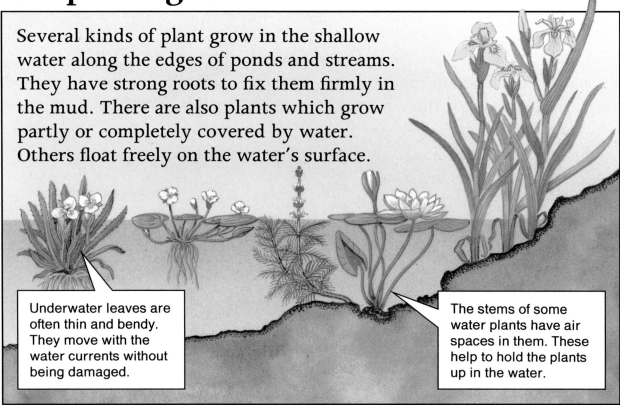

Underwater leaves are often thin and bendy. They move with the water currents without being damaged.

The stems of some water plants have air spaces in them. These help to hold the plants up in the water.

Which plants grow in the sea?

All plants that grow in the sea are types of algae. They range in size from microscopic specks to enormous seaweeds, up to 200 feet long. The three main types of seaweed are different colors—red, brown, and green.

? DO YOU KNOW

Many seaweeds have air-filled bladders to keep them afloat, and a branched foot called a holdfast to fix them to the rocks.

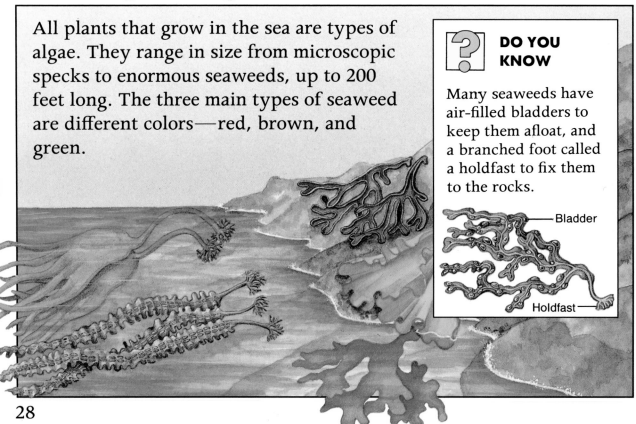

Bladder

Holdfast

Can plants grow without water?

No plant can live entirely without water, but many desert plants can survive long periods of drought. They often have spreading roots to reach every available drop of water, and a waxy outer skin to cut down water loss. Many store water in their bodies—some cactus stems can hold more than 25 gallons! The seeds of desert plants may lie in the ground for years. But after a rainstorm they burst into flower.

Within days of a shower, desert flowers burst into life. They soon die, leaving their seeds to wait for rain.

The barrel cactus is named for its shape. Its juicy flesh has provided water for many thirsty travelers.

MAKE A MINI-DESERT

Sow a packet of mixed cactus seeds in a shallow tray filled with a mixture of one part sand and two parts compost. Keep the seeds warm and moist to start them off. Don't overwater the plants.

Cacti don't like having wet roots

The Old Man cactus has a coat of white hair which protects it from hot sun and freezing nights.

What grows in the rainforests?

Tropical rainforests contain around half of all the living things on Earth. They are always hot and wet, and growing conditions are ideal for all kinds of plants— plant trees, woody creepers, beautiful orchids, shrubs, ferns, and mosses. Trees grow so thickly in most parts of the forest that their tops form a dense leafy roof called the canopy. Most plants grow and flower in the canopy—it's dark and gloomy below.

A few giant trees grow higher than 160 feet and poke their heads through the canopy.

Many trees grow so thickly that their tops form a shady roof called the canopy.

It's dark and gloomy below the canopy, but some plants get enough light to grow.

Mosses, fungi, and ferns grow among the rotting leaves on the ground.

DO YOU KNOW

The tropical rain-forests of the world are being chopped down and burned at an alarming rate. An area the size of a football field is cut down each second. About 50 plant species are lost every day.

Can plants grow in the snow?

No plants can survive in the very coldest parts of the world where there is snow all year round. But a number of species manage to grow in areas where they are covered in snow for as long as nine months of the year. They have to flower very quickly when spring arrives, so they can make their seeds before winter comes around again.

DO YOU KNOW

Treeline

Some trees can survive quite high up on mountainsides if there is enough water and good soil. But there is a point above which the conditions are too poor for trees to grow. This is the tree-line.

The leaves of the edelweiss have a thick coat of hair which traps heat and cuts down water loss.

The Alpine soldanella uses its food stores to keep it warm. It can produce enough heat to melt the snow.

Moss campion lives for a long time. It may wait ten years before flowering for the first time.

Lichen is a type of plant which can survive long droughts and extreme cold, but it grows very slowly.

Which plants do we eat?

All the food we eat comes either from plants or from animals that eat plants. And many different parts of plants are useful to us. We eat hundreds of different fruits, of course, but we also eat the roots of plants such as carrot and turnip, and the stems of celery and asparagus. Cabbage and lettuce are eaten mainly for their leaves, while corn, rice and wheat are grown for their seeds. When we eat broccoli we are eating flowers!

Huge machines called combine harvesters cut the wheat and separate the seeds from the stalks.

 FOOD FACTS

The food we eat today comes from all over the world. Potatoes once grew only in the Andes of South America, for example. Here's a list of some of the things we eat and their original homes.

Apples – Europe
Bananas – S. Asia
Grapes – W. Asia
Mangoes – India
Oranges – China
Tomatoes – S. America

The world's biggest producers of wheat are China and the Soviet Union, followed by the United States.

A number of animals live among the wheat plants. Fieldmice build their homes on the stalks.

The seeds are loaded into trucks and taken away to the flour mill to be cleaned and ground into flour.

GROW YOUR OWN FOOD

Cress and mustard are easy to grow and good to eat in sandwiches or with salads.

1 Sprinkle some cress and mustard seeds over a piece of blotting paper on a saucer.

2 Put the saucer in a warm light place and keep the paper damp. You should see the results in a few days!

Flour is used to make bread, breakfast cereal, pasta, as well as cookies and other food.

Which plants do we drink?

Many different drinks are made from plants, including two of the world's most popular ones—tea and coffee. Beer is made mainly from barley, while almost all wine comes from grapes. Cola drinks are flavored with cola nuts—the seeds of a West African tree. Many other soft drinks are made from different kinds of fruit juice.

Chocolate and cocoa are made from the dried beans of the Cacao tree (below). This small bushy tree grows in warm, moist parts of Africa and South America.

Cacao bean

The leaves are plucked by machines in flat areas. But in hilly places, the tea is hand-picked.

Tea comes from the leaves of a bush which grows in warm places. India produces most of the world's tea.

The leaves are taken to a nearby factory where they are left to rot slightly before being dried.

Coffee is made from the beans of the coffee plant (below). The beans develop inside fleshy red berries. They are dried, roasted, and ground to make coffee powder.

Coffee bean

How is cotton made?

Cotton is made from the hairlike fibers that surround the seeds of the cotton plant. It has a huge number of uses—from clothes and carpets, to rope and even paper. The seeds and fibers develop inside a fruit called a boll. After the bolls are picked and dried, the long soft fibers are separated from the seeds and then spun and woven into cloth.

 DO YOU KNOW

Other parts of the cotton plant are useful, beside the fibers. Cottonseed oil is made by squeezing the seeds. It's used to make soap, as well as food products such as salad oil and margarine. The seeds have short fuzzy hairs which are used to stuff mattresses and cushions, and to make paper and plastics.

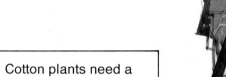

Cotton plants need a long sunny growing season, with about 180 frost-free days.

Cotton cloth is strong and hard-wearing. It is easy to wash and comfortable to wear.

A typical cotton boll is about the same size as a golf ball and contains up to 500,000 fibers. The boll splits open when it is ripe.

Which were the first plants?

Plants are the oldest form of life on Earth. Our planet is thought to be about 4.6 billion years old, and the first plants appeared 3 billion years ago. They were single-celled algae which lived in warm shallow water. Over 1.5 billion years passed before the first plants grew on land.

By the time of the dinosaurs, 225 million years ago, the land was covered in swampy forests of cycad and conifer trees, and giant horsetails and ferns. Flowering plants appeared last of all—over 100 million years later.

DO YOU KNOW

Coal is the remains of the swampy forests that covered the Earth millions of years ago. As the plants died, they sank to the bottom of the swamps. More plants grew on top, squashing the dead ones into layers, which eventually turned into hard coal.

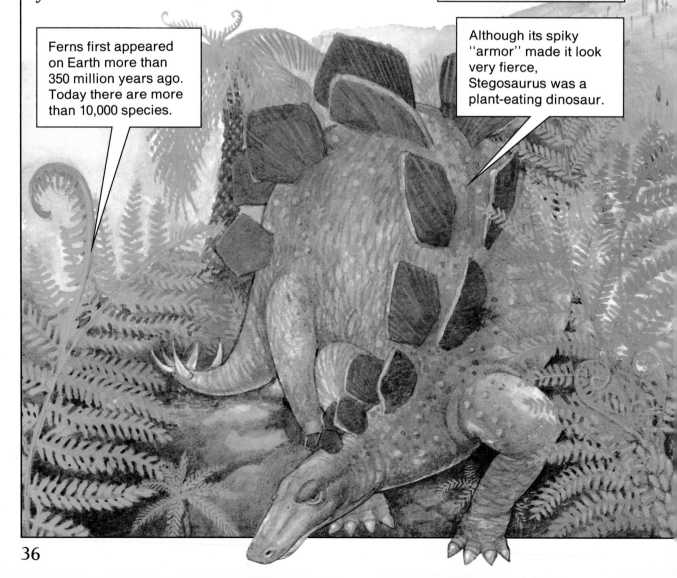

Ferns first appeared on Earth more than 350 million years ago. Today there are more than 10,000 species.

Although its spiky "armor" made it look very fierce, Stegosaurus was a plant-eating dinosaur.

There were forests of evergreen conifer trees, which provided food for the plant-eating dinosaurs.

Cycads looked like small palm trees with fat trunks. There are about 100 species left on Earth today.

DO YOU KNOW

The gingko or maidenhair tree grows in China and has hardly changed in the last 150 million years. Other living fossils include horsetail and cycad species, which are very similar to their ancient relatives.

Horsetails grew to be enormous—some were up to 60 feet high! Only a few small species survive today.

Why do some plants die out?

Over the centuries, many plant species have died out naturally. Nowadays, a large number of plants are threatened by people. Clearing fields and woods to build houses kills plants, as do the poisonous gases given off by cars and factories. Once only a few plants are left, careless picking can make a species disappear forever.

The bellflower is very rare in the wild, but its popularity with gardeners should stop it from disappearing.

The Cheddar pink only grows in Britain, France, and Switzerland. It may die out if people keep picking it.

The Holy Ghost orchid is dying out because the areas where it grows are being destroyed.

Useful words?

Cell   The smallest living unit, and the building block from which all plants and animals are made. Some living things are just a single cell. Others are made of many – an adult human has about 50 billion cells! Cells are so small that they can only be seen under a microscope.

Chlorophyll   A special green substance that gives plants their color. Chlorophyll allows plants to capture the energy in sunlight and use it to make food.

Deciduous   Deciduous trees shed all their leaves each year in the fall. They have bare branches through the winter and grow new leaves in spring.

Evergreen   Evergreen trees don't shed all their leaves at once, and their branches are never completely bare. These trees lose old leaves and grow new ones a few at a time throughout the year.

Fertilization   The joining together of a pollen grain and an egg. A new seed starts to grow after the egg is fertilized.

Germination   When a seed starts to sprout and grow. Seeds germinate when they have enough water and warmth. The first root appears and grows downward, then the first shoot pushes its way up through the soil.

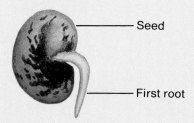

Seed

First root

Photosynthesis   The process whereby plants use the energy in sunlight to turn water from the soil and carbon dioxide from the air into a sugary food. The word photosynthesis means "building with light."

Reproduction   The word reproduce means "make again," and reproduction is the process of making a new plant or animal.

Some plants reproduce by sending out side shoots called runners. Roots form where they touch the ground, and a new plant grows.

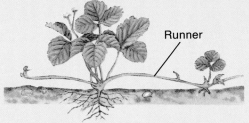

Runner

Sap   The juices inside the stem of a plant. Sap is made up of water and the sugary food which plants make in their leaves. The food is carried in sap to all parts of the plant.

Seed   A small capsule containing a baby plant and a store of food to give the young plant a start in life. Flowering plants reproduce by making seeds.

Species   A group of the same kind of plant. An oak is a species of tree, for example. Willows, elms, pines, and firs are also trees, but each one is a different species.

Spore   A single tiny cell which grows into a new plant. Non-flowering plants such as algae, ferns, and mosses, reproduce by making spores.

Index?

A
alga 4–5, 26, 36, 39
Alpine soldanella 31
animal 4, 11, 13, 16, 17, 21, 27, 32

B
Baobab tree 22
Banyan tree 22
bark 19, 20, 21
Barrel cactus 29
Bellflower 38
Birch catkin 10
Bracket fungus 27
Brazilian duckweed 6
bread 27, 33
Bristlecone pine 20
bromeliad 9
bulb 15

C
Cacao tree 34
cactus 17, 29
carbon dioxide 8, 39
carpel 10
cell 5, 26, 39
Chanterelle mushroom 27
Cheddar pink 38
chlorophyll 8, 27, 39
chocolate 24, 34
coal 36
coco-de-mer 12
cocoa 34
coconut 23
coffee 24, 34
conifer 36, 37
corm 15
corn 4, 32
cotton 35
crocus 15
cycad 36, 37

D
daffodil 15
deciduous 18, 39
desert 4, 17, 29

E
Edelweiss 31
egg 10, 11, 12
epiphyte 9
eucalyptus 7, 20
evergreen 18, 39

F
fern 5, 26, 30, 36, 39
fertilization 10, 11, 13, 39

flower 5, 10, 11, 15, 21, 39
flowering plants 4–5, 36, 39
Fly agaric toadstool 27
fruit 12, 13, 21, 22, 24, 32
fungus 27

G
germination 14, 39
Giant puff-ball 27
Giant saguaro 29
Giant sequoia 7
gingko see maidenhair tree
grasses 4

H
Holy Ghost orchid 38
honey possum 11
horsetail 26, 36, 37

I
iris 15

J
Jackfruit 12

L
leaf 5, 6, 8, 14, 15, 18–19, 21, 26, 28, 31, 39
lichen 31

M
maidenhair tree 37
Mangrove tree 23
meat-eating plant 16
mimosa 17
Montezuma cypress 7
moss 4, 26, 30, 39
Moss campion 31
mountain 4, 31
mudskipper 23
mushroom 27

N
nectar 11
nettle 17
non-flowering plants 4–5, 26, 39
nut 12, 24

O
oak 19, 21
Old Man cactus 29
orchid 9, 30
ovary 10, 12
oxygen 8, 19, 23

P
palm tree 6, 19, 23

paper 24–25, 35
penicillin 27
photosynthesis 8, 19, 39
pitcher plant 16
pollen 10, 11, 12
potato 15
puff-ball 27

R
Raffia palm 6
Rafflesia 6
rainforest 30
reproduction 5, 15, 39
rhizome 15
rice 4, 32
root 5, 8, 9, 14, 18, 19, 20, 21, 23, 26, 28, 29, 32, 39
rubber 25
runner 15, 39

S
sap 8, 21, 25, 39
seaweed 5, 26, 28
seed 5, 10, 14, 26, 29, 30, 39
species 4–5, 39
spore 5, 26, 39
stamen 10, 11
Stapelia 11
stem 5, 8, 15, 19, 26, 28
stigma 10, 11
stomata 8
strawberry 15
style 10
Sundew 16

T
tea 35
timber 24–25
toadstool 27
tree 4–5, 7, 18–19, 20, 21, 24–25, 26, 30, 31, 39
treeline 31
trunk 7, 19, 20, 22

V
Venus flytrap 16
Victoria water-lily 6

W
water 8, 18–19, 28, 39
water plants 28
wheat 4, 32–33
wood 24–25

X
xylem 8